SPIRIT ANIMALS

SPIRIT ANIMALS

*Unlocking the Secrets of
Our Animal Companions*

By Stefanie Iris Weiss

Illustrations by
Lisa Congdon, Kyle Field, Grady McFerrin,
Julie Morstad, Christopher Silas Neal,
Clare Rojas, Rachel Salomon,
Hannah Stouffer, and Betsy Walton

CHRONICLE BOOKS
SAN FRANCISCO

Illustrations by:
Lisa Congdon, pp. 18, 65, 77, 78, 89
Kyle Field, pp. 42, 61
Grady McFerrin, pp. 21, 37, 49, 73
Julie Morstad, pp. 22, 29, 45, 74, 97
Christopher Silas Neal, pp. 34, 58, 69, 90
Clare Rojas, pp. 38, 46, 53, 66, 70
Rachel Salomon, pp. 30, 33, 54, 81, 93
Hannah Stouffer, pp. 25, 41, 50, 82, 86
Betsy Walton, pp. 26, 57, 62, 85, 94

Library of Congress Cataloging-in-Publication Data available.

ISBN: 978-0-8118-6843-3

Manufactured in China

Designed by Kristen Hewitt

10 9 8 7 6 5 4 3 2 1

Chronicle Books LLC
680 Second Street
San Francisco, California 94107

www.chroniclebooks.com

CONTENTS

INTRODUCTION

ANIMAL MAGNETISM

In our hyper-industrialized, polluted, and plugged-in culture, we're often too busy to connect with our deeper selves, let alone find time to walk our dogs through the park without obsessively checking our cell phones. Instead, many of us rush to work and hire someone else to walk Fido. We rarely connect face-to-face and instant message our way through the day, living much of our lives online. It's no wonder we're so disoriented and cut off from one another. Finding your spirit animal is a way to take a moment to breathe, reconnect, and remember what it means to be a human, not a robot. Your spirit animal can help reveal what your purpose is. If you're in need of guidance, healing, or protection, you just might find it with one of the animals illustrated in this book.

There is absolute power and mystery in our animal companions: We see it in a cat's mesmeric eyes or a dog's wagging tail. And the pets we love and live with just seem to "get" us (see the entries for Dog and Cat). But what about the animals that live wilder lives? What do we modern folks have to learn from them? This book will be the beginning of a revealing journey for those of us who usually get no closer to wild animals than watching them on TV or the occasional trip to the zoo. Whether in flesh or spirit, animals have much to teach us.

A BIT OF HISTORY

From the Aborigines of Australia to Native Americans, Greco-Roman citizens, Northern Europeans, South Asians, and beyond, spirit or "power" animals have played an important role in myriad cultures. Because these ancient cultures were attuned to the natural world, of necessity, they tapped into the primordial power of the spirit animal realm. Man was one with nature in many of these traditions, and people were unafraid of stepping into "non-ordinary reality": the stuff of dreams, shamanic journeys, and deep meditation. In fact, these types of activities were fundamental to their lives.

We've only just begun to catch up with the genius of these ancient people. Carl Jung believed that people all over the world are intimately linked via the *collective unconscious*—the inherited part of our unconscious mind, a universal human "bathtub" that holds the memories, experiences, and wisdom of the entire human race. When you dream or meditate, you tap into this vast network of the imagination, going back thousands of years. Establishing a connection with spirit animals is a direct link to this innate wisdom.

WHERE THE WILD THINGS ARE

The collective unconscious knows no bounds—spirit animals exist on every continent. For Native American shamans, spirit animals provide spiritual medicine for the lost and bereft. Shamans believe that, unlike totem animals, spirit animals often change across one's lifetime, according to need. In India, many of the sacred myths of Hinduism rely on the power and presence of animals. Perhaps the most famous of these is Ganesha, the elephant god believed to be a banisher of obstacles. In Norse tradition, Odin rode an eight-legged steed across the sky and into the realm of death. The Australian Aboriginal creation myth centers on a rainbow serpent that birthed the land and its people. And in Japan, Shinto shrines dedicated to dogs, foxes, and monkeys can be found all over the country.

COSMIC CHANGES

The earth is going through radical transformations, and we're all feeling it in our very bones. From climate change to the rash of natural and man-made disasters in recent years, something major is afoot. Astrologers have been predicting these upheavals for years: From approximately 2008 to 2023, Pluto will be in Capricorn, a powerful earth sign. This is a harbinger of tremendous change—the last time Pluto was in Capricorn, the Revolutionary War occurred. But before we can repair our planet and all of its systems, both man-made and natural, we must attend to our inner lives.

Having a spirit animal companion is a direct route to a place where the air is always clean and the sea and soil are pristine.

Some people call their priest, rabbi, guru, or therapist when in need of a little spiritual wisdom or earthly advice. Your spirit animal is like your own personal, internal guru, and dialing it up is easier than getting an appointment with an analyst. Plus, it's free.

HOW TO USE THIS BOOK

If you're new to the concept of spirit animals, the first thing to understand is that you don't necessarily choose your animal—you and your animal choose each other. The animals are spirit teachers that dwell in our unconscious mind, waiting for us to discover them. Before reading the descriptions in the book, leaf through the pages and linger on any images that strike you as welcoming or meaningful. You might find that one particular image feels like it "belongs" to you. At this point, read the text. Does that animal's description fit your needs right now? If so, you may have found your spirit animal. Unlike other resources on this topic, this book focuses on the "right here, right now" animal, not the totem animal that comes and stays with you for life. You might find and meet that permanent spirit guardian here, but the book is organized so that the animals can go to work for you on specific problems you're encountering right now. And the spirit animals have been listed alphabetically, so you can find the one you're looking for with ease.

Say you've been dreaming, for instance, of owls; consider that a calling from the spiritual realm. Even if the corresponding text doesn't speak to you at this moment, wait a bit. Something may be coming into your life that will require the wisdom of the owl. Some people find that shortly before or after discovering the concept of spirit animals they begin to see signs everywhere. A man in need of an important career change may see a series of butterflies during his commute and butterfly tattoos that he never noticed before on his coworkers. When this type of synchronicity occurs, you'll know that transformation is in the works. If the neighborhood stray cat has chosen your yard or windowsill as its new hangout, perhaps it's time to start thinking about independence and where it's lacking in your life. Ignore signs from the animal realm at your peril. They've likely come to you for good reasons: protection and nurturing. If you've been encountering a certain animal over and over, it may be time to take a deeper look at what it's trying to tell you. Some people believe that their angels hover in close proximity, on call in case of crisis. Your spirit animal serves the same purpose, but it has the potential to lead you down an even more enlightening path.

If you received this book as a gift, you may question whether it has any purpose in your life. For you, it may be wise to use the book as an oracle of sorts. Simply close your eyes, take a deep breath, and flip through the pages until you feel compelled to stop. If you feel a resonance with the animal you've been led to, there is probably a reason. Think of this activity like a tarot card reading: The delicate, subtle energies running through you helped you to arrive at this page; it most likely wasn't arbitrary. You can also ask the book a question. Take a deep breath and say, for instance, "When will I find love?" And then flip through. Whichever animal you land upon may provide the answers you seek, if you listen closely enough.

If you already feel connected to a particular animal, read about it here to learn more about its history and personality. And know that you can always add more to your animal arsenal, depending on the challenges you face.

This book is organized as follows: Each animal is named and given a moniker, which sums up its strength and purpose. Next, "Personality" describes each animal's real-world behaviors. If you stumbled upon your animal in the forest, it would likely be doing these very deeds. In this section, you'll also find information about where your spirit animal might be found in the real world. "Spiritual Origins" summarizes key cultural and historical information about the animal, explaining its significance within various traditions. "Guiding Powers" explains how the animal can help you spiritually (and practically) if you choose to call upon it for guidance. Finally, at the bottom of the page you'll find information on "Companion Animals," or those animals with similar or complementary traits. We've included forty animals in this book, but any of the thousands in the animal kingdom could one day be your spirit animal guide. We chose these forty based upon the needs of people in today's world, with its particular brand of challenges.

DREAMING AND MEDITATION

If simply flipping through this book isn't providing the answers you seek, you may need to go deeper. We all sleep and dream each night, and you can use this necessary downtime as a way to explore the astral realm, as a bridge to the unconscious. If you typically fall into bed, exhausted, after a long day and tune in to the television, start by making bedtime more of a healthy ritual. Lower the lights at least an hour before you're due to turn in, to slowly unwind, or take a hot shower or bath to relax your body. Leave a notebook and pen by your bedside. As you drift off, invite your would-be spirit animal to visit you in your dreams. When you wake up, immediately write down your dreams in the notebook. Even if the animal doesn't appear the first night, it will come soon enough.

Visualization is an important tool when trying to contact your spirit animal guide. If you'd prefer to find your guide while awake, go to a quiet, private spot, preferably outside, where you won't be bothered. Sit on the ground or in a chair, and center yourself, with eyes closed. Take three deep breaths, and imagine yourself in a forest, a desert, on a mountaintop, or in some other completely natural setting. See yourself there, walking and exploring the territory. Stay as long as you can, all the while keeping your mind open to whatever animals might choose to visit you on this journey. Be patient; you may not meet your guide the first time. Meditation takes practice, but it's extremely rewarding. There are as many ways to meet your spirit animal guide as there are animals in the wild. There is no "right" path. Be patient with yourself, and learn to tune into your unconscious.

SAMPLE MEDITATIONS
If you're not sure which animal to work with, use this meditation:

Right here, right now, I am reaching out for what I need. I may not know exactly what that is yet, but you do. Whatever shape you take, I open my mind and body to your spiritual wisdom. I want to see you, feel you, smell you, and understand you. I want to explore your habitat so you can fill my world with the healing and pure power that you possess. You are the next step on my path.

If you have already chosen an animal, gaze at its image, read its description, and chant or silently read the following:

I invite you into my life (insert animal's name here). I crave your energy. Everything I've done up to now has led to this moment. I'm reaching deep into the collective unconscious so I can see you, feel you, touch you, and smell you. I'm ready for the wisdom only you can provide.

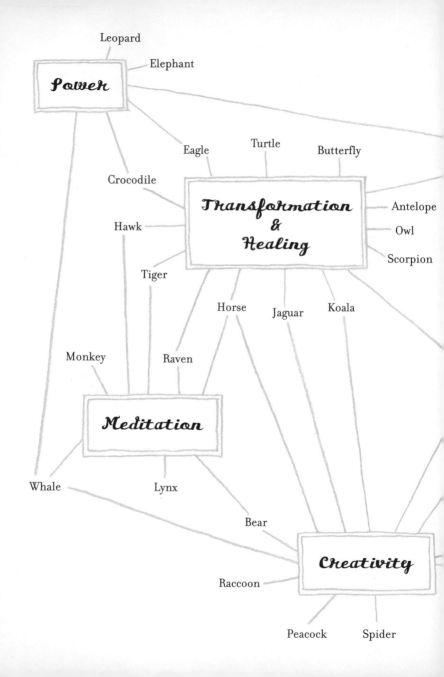

MAP OF
SPIRITUAL STRENGTHS

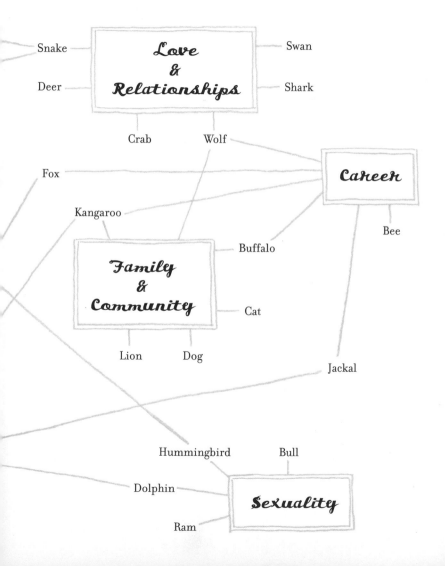

THE
ANIMALS

ANTELOPE
The Gentle Survivor

PERSONALITY

Antelope are horned creatures with cattlelike hooves and are usually found
in mountainous terrain. They're indigenous to Africa and Eurasia and are
now found in the Americas. They know how to survive even in the harshest of
environments. Both male and female antelope are lovely to look at, possessing
a feminine softness that conceals a fierce power to survive brutal conditions.
Every cautious, graceful step they take up an inaccessible-to-most mountain-
side shows us that strength can be beautiful.

SPIRITUAL ORIGINS

These sleek, swift, and agile animals show us how to make lemonade out of
life's lemons. Due to its survival instincts, the antelope is the symbol for
Capricorn—the sign of strength and will—in the Hindu zodiac. The antelope
was also the emblem of Shiva in India. In Egyptian mythology, the antelope was
sacred to the goddess Isis, who famously sewed together the remnants of her
brother/husband Osiris's body after he was killed. She was a great, strong
heroine to her people.

GUIDING POWERS

The antelope is the ideal spirit animal in times of crisis. If you're struggling to
achieve something but hitting constant roadblocks, the antelope can show you
the way to your goal. When you feel yourself starting to give up, the antelope
will help you understand why it's worth going back to the drawing board. The
antelope will lead you all the way to the mountaintop.

COMPANION ANIMALS
Elephant *(strength)* and Swan *(grace)*

BEAR
The Patient Pillar

PERSONALITY
The bear is not a violent animal by nature. It's only when we infringe upon its territory or threaten its young that it will unleash its ferocity. The bear is also not a spontaneous animal: A bear cub will remain with its mother for seven years, learning the laws of the land. And the bear plans far in advance for its winter hibernation. Bears are found in North America, South America, Europe, Asia, and the Arctic.

SPIRITUAL ORIGINS
The bear is revered by cultures all over the world, including lands as disparate as Siberia, Finland, and Japan. Whether black, polar, brown, grizzly, or a more exotic variety, all bears share strength, stamina, and patience. Known as "Dog of God" to the Finns, the bear is believed in Finland to be ten times as powerful as man and twelve times more intelligent. In Japan, bears are understood to represent wisdom and compassion. Some Native American shamans believe the bear symbolizes the awakening of the unconscious mind. The constellation Ursa Major was named after the bear because of the animal's power.

GUIDING POWERS
Bears teach us how to bring dreams into reality. They tend to move slowly (unless in hot pursuit of prey), and they teach us to take time when searching for inner wisdom. If you're feeling a creative block, consider the counsel of this spirit animal. The bear will show you how to remove yourself from daily stress and how to get truly quiet. No artistic challenge can be met in the midst of distraction, chaos, and confusion. The bear will help you to create your masterpiece by providing the clarity of vision one can only achieve in silence.

COMPANION ANIMALS
Spider *(illusion)* and Tiger *(solitude)*

BEE
The Industrious Collaborator

PERSONALITY

Honeybees, bumblebees, and stingless bees live in social groups with strict divisions of labor. Bees are known for their pack mentality, work ethic, and devotion to their queen. They're all about getting the job done, and they rarely sting unless provoked. Bees diligently collect nectar and pollinate flowers—patience and an extremely focused spirit are their gifts. They remind us of the power of service. Bees are found on every continent, except for Antarctica.

SPIRITUAL ORIGINS

Because honey was one of the first foods and preservatives of many ancient cultures, the bee has achieved high spiritual status all over the world: The Egyptian sun god Ra's tears were imagined as bees. In India, the Hindu gods Vishnu, Indra, and Krishna were considered "nectar-born ones," or *madhava*. (Krishna is often symbolized with a blue bee on his forehead.) In Greek mythology, both Zeus and Dionysus were fed by bees as babies. And Aristotle believed that good souls would reincarnate as bees—in fact, many cultures see bees as messengers of the gods and symbols of the human soul.

GUIDING POWERS

The bee is the ideal spirit animal when you're stressing about a project and need to get organized, especially when you're working with others on a deadline. If your colleagues refuse to cooperate with you, the bee makes an excellent counselor. The bee teaches determination and patience: It'll lead you step by step to your goal and help you find the patience to deal with even the most intransigent coworker.

COMPANION ANIMALS
Hawk *(clarity)* and Raccoon *(resourcefulness)*

BUFFALO
The Gracious Provider

PERSONALITY

Wild buffalo will attack if they feel threatened; they are extremely protective of their companions. The buffalo's strong shoulders are its storehouse of power, but its sheer size and powerful presence will usually cause other animals to keep their distance. Domesticated buffalo quickly adapt to new environments—they are often used as dairy animals and provide humans with much sustenance. Buffalo are indigenous to North America, Asia, Europe, Africa, and the Middle East.

SPIRITUAL ORIGINS

Many Native American tribes consider the buffalo the chief of all animals, a sacred animal that represents the earth. Rare, white buffalo are especially praised. In other cultures, the Hindu warrior goddess Durga was sent by the gods to slay a buffalo monster, and legend has it that Chinese philosopher Lao-tzu left China riding a water buffalo.

GUIDING POWERS

Generosity, strength, and abundance are at the heart of the buffalo's teaching. They remind us of the need for gratitude, by showing us that when we give, we always receive. The buffalo shows us how to be thankful for what we have in scarce times. Feeling stressed about money? This is the ideal spirit animal to show you the path to wealth: According to the buffalo, prosperity begins with your own herd; allocate your resources and you'll always be provided for. True wealth comes to those who are unafraid to share their treasures.

COMPANION ANIMALS
Kangaroo *(abundance)* and Antelope *(perseverance)*

BULL
The Defiant Lover

PERSONALITY

The bull's strength, virility, and power are evident—this is why humans have used it as a helping animal since the early Neolithic period. Getting a bull to move is not an easy task, though. These animals are definitely lovers, not fighters. They are entirely self-indulgent creatures that, left to their own devices, will graze on grass, relax in meadows, and mate with cows all day long. Bulls are found on every continent, except for Antarctica.

SPIRITUAL ORIGINS

The bull is the symbol of the constellation of Taurus, an earth sign ruling the five senses and one's relationship with the natural world. Hindus revere the cow (the female version of a bull) and see it as a symbol of strength and reproductive power. Cows still roam the streets of India; they are deeply venerated, even anointed and painted during festivals. In Celtic mythology, the bull represented potency and good fortune. The Scandinavians believed that Nerthus, the Earth Mother, was pulled across the land by sacred cows once a year.

GUIDING POWERS

Are you dealing with a troubled or lackluster love life? The bull will help you to fully understand the underlying issues. It's all about virility with this highly sensual animal. If sexual repression is a problem for you or your lover, the bull will pull you both along, getting you back in touch with what feels good and natural.

COMPANION ANIMALS
Dolphin (*joy*) and Ram (*virility*)

BUTTERFLY
The Delicate Transformer

PERSONALITY

Butterflies fly only during the day and drink nectar from flowers for sustenance. These beautiful creatures emerge from their far less attractive larval stage to dot the landscape with magical bursts of color. Most live for only two weeks, showing us how fleeting life can be. They are gentle and lovely but incredibly powerful within. Able to focus their intention and create majestic wings out of the stillness of an unassuming cocoon, they explode into the world and make magic. Butterflies are found on every continent, except for Antarctica.

SPIRITUAL ORIGINS

The beauty of a butterfly in flight mesmerizes even the most jaded onlooker. In China and Japan, the butterfly is a symbol of immortality and joy. The ancient Greek word for butterfly is *psyche*, which also means "soul." The Greek *Horae*, or goddesses of the seasons, were often depicted with butterfly wings. And some Native American tribes view the butterfly not only as a symbol of beauty, grace, and happiness, but also of transformation and shape-shifting.

GUIDING POWERS

The butterfly is your spirit animal when you're ready for a change. If you know that you need a revolution right here and right now, call upon the butterfly. It will show you that only you can truly transform yourself; no external force can get you to the next level. The butterfly will lead you down the path of creative indwelling, removing any fear of being alone for as long as it takes you to become the true version of yourself. Remember Ghandi's message—be the change you want to see in the world. The butterfly will get you there.

COMPANION ANIMALS
Fox (*shape-shifting*) and Raven (*magic*)

CAT
The Independent Protector

PERSONALITY

Cats can be found all over the world. These sleek, sexy creatures are not all about cuddling and coddling—the cat does what it wants when it wants. At the same time, cats and their humans share a bond of trust and love that can't be broken. Witness a house cat, rich with all the amenities of modern life, hunting toy mice and leaving them at the foot of its owner's bed as an offering. They own their humans, and this arrangement works out for all of us. Cats are our stealth protectors; they don't bark at intruders like dogs do, but their body language tells us everything we need to know about anyone who walks through the door.

SPIRITUAL ORIGINS

Known as a cult animal in ancient Egypt, domestic cats have been part of the human family for at least 9,500 years. The Egyptian goddess Bast was often shown in cat form as the protector of home and hearth, and the temple cats of Bast were mummified and buried as royalty. Black cats were especially lucky for Egyptians; physicians advertised their services with a black cat emblem. Families mourned when their house cats died: family members would shave their eyebrows. And in the Norse tradition, Freyja—the goddess of love, fertility, and beauty—is often shown riding a chariot pulled by cats.

GUIDING POWERS

Whether there's a real live cat in your life or not, the spirit of the cat can comfort you when domestic life has grown mundane. Independence is the cat's primary lesson. If you need to get away from the routine of a relationship that feels stale, borrow from the mystical arsenal of the cat. If you're not ready to leave a partnership but need space, the cat proves a great example. The cat will bring the necessary magic and mystery back to your life.

COMPANION ANIMALS
Snake *(magic)* and Horse *(autonomy)*

CRAB
The Fierce Feminine

PERSONALITY

Crabs will protect themselves by using their sharp claws when threatened. Their tough exterior contains a soft, fleshy, and undeniably vulnerable underbelly. Whatever tactics crabs use in self-defense are necessary. They move by intuition, walking sideways and using all of their senses to protect themselves and their young. Crabs are found in all of the oceans of the world.

SPIRITUAL ORIGINS

According to Greek legend, the goddess Hera placed a huge crab in the sky to create the constellation of Cancer. This fourth sign of the zodiac represents motherhood, security, and all things related to home. Cancer symbolism extends to self-protection and sensitivity, indicating the soft interior and hard shell of the crab. Cancer is a moody, emotional sign, so we know why we feel "crabby" on certain occasions.

GUIDING POWERS

Both men and women can benefit from the advocacy of the crab's fierce feminine power. The crab will help you to heal your relationship with your mother, or anyone who has been (or wants to be) a nurturer for you. This creature will share its soulful wisdom without sidestepping. You'll never again neglect the need for self-preservation. If you're struggling with issues of fertility, the crab will put you in touch with your own inner mother and show you how to protect and defend your young, both literally and metaphorically. Intuition is the lifeblood of the crab; it will show you how to listen to your gut again.

COMPANION ANIMALS
Deer (*support*) and Koala (*attunement with self*)

CROCODILE
The Primordial Powerhouse

PERSONALITY

Close relatives of the dinosaur, crocodiles have survived almost unchanged for 65 million years. While stalking prey, crocs will stealthily skim their watery habitat, with just their eyes visible, and then attack with terrifying ferocity. Crocodiles are above any emotion; all that matters are their basic needs. Their gaping jaws and huge, sharp teeth put all other animals on notice—that is, if they have time to gaze upon the croc before it strikes. Crocodiles are found in Africa, Asia, the Americas, and Australia.

SPIRITUAL ORIGINS

Crocodiles were venerated as gods in ancient Egypt. They had a dual nature: They were thought to bring the rains, which fed the crops and created the harvest. But at the same time, they were deeply feared. Crocs were also associated with the god of evil, Set. The Romans revered the crocodile for its stealth, silence, and mystery. And many cultures see crocodiles as keepers of primordial wisdom.

GUIDING POWERS

If you need to get to the root of a problem that feels like it should have been resolved a million years ago, consult the crocodile. Old patterns, especially those stemming from unresolved parental issues, may be met head on with the counsel of the crocodile. The croc will show you the true power of your ancestry and help you to leave behind the stuff that you no longer need, by showing you how to get back to the basics. Before you can be fully present or even look toward the future, you must confront the past head on. The crocodile will help you to be truthful with yourself without neurosis or hypersensitivity.

COMPANION ANIMALS
Crab *(instinct)*, Jaguar *(liberation)*, and Whale *(wisdom)*

DEER
The Sensitive Listener

PERSONALITY

The quiet and delicate deer appears to us as a sweet and harmless forest creature. Unlike antelope, the deer's sister species, deer shed and regrow their antlers each year. Whether stag, doe, or fawn, deer are rarely feared by humans. They can be found sitting near campsites and observing our rituals with rapt attention. Deer are indigenous to all continents, except for Antarctica and Australia.

SPIRITUAL ORIGINS

The Celts called deer "fairy cattle"; they were thought of as messengers. In India, Vayu, the god of the wind, rode on a deer. In the Hindu Upanishads, Saraswati, the goddess of learning, took the form of a deer. To the Shintoists of Japan, the deer is considered a messenger of the gods. And the Huichol people of Mexico see the "magical deer" as a symbol of both sustenance and enlightenment.

GUIDING POWERS

When you need to be heard and nurtured, call upon the deer as your spirit animal. If you're being too hard on yourself or if someone in your life is treating you poorly, this animal will bring you back to balance and give you the courage to speak your mind. Calm and centeredness come when the deer is invited into your life. Think of the deer's antlers as antennae, tuned into the subtle energies that swirl through your unconscious. Your powers of extra-sensory perception can be stimulated by the presence of the deer, especially in delicate relationship matters when you need to listen to your gut.

COMPANION ANIMALS
Crab (*instinct*) and Lynx (*trust*)

DOG
The Loyal Companion

PERSONALITY

The dog earned the moniker "man's best friend" because of its respect and undying love for its master. The infinite devotion is evident—a loyal dog follows us around the house, howls when we leave, and will fiercely protect us from interlopers. Found throughout the world, dogs are the most easily trained domestic animal, and they don't begrudge us for telling them how to behave.

SPIRITUAL ORIGINS

In Hindu tradition, dogs guard the door of heaven as messengers of Yama, god of death. In Chinese astrology, the dog is thought of as honest, intelligent, loyal, and straightforward. In Japan, the dog is known as a protector and guardian. In Homer's *Odyssey*, Argos was Odysseus's loyal hound; he waited dutifully for Odysseus to return from his long trip, almost dying in the process out of love for his master. Dogs were long associated with the Great Mother goddess of the pre-Christian era. They are deeply connected to incarnations of Artemis the huntress.

GUIDING POWERS

During times of loneliness or abandonment, the dog is a friend indeed. This is the ideal spirit animal when you're feeling disconnected from family or friends and in need of camaraderie. If you've been hurt by someone that you once believed in, the dog can help you to regain your ability to trust.

COMPANION ANIMALS
Wolf (*community*) and Kangaroo (*trust*)

DOLPHIN
The Playful Genius

PERSONALITY
Dolphins are social animals that live in pods or schools of up to a dozen members. They are the geniuses of the sea; researchers have found that some species of dolphins teach their young to use tools. They engage in foreplay—sex is not just about reproduction for these creatures. Dolphins communicate with clicks, whistles, and other vocalizations. They play and play-fight with other dolphins and often seem to show off by making acrobatic leaps out of the water. Dolphins are found in oceans worldwide, mainly in the shallower seas of the continental shelves.

SPIRITUAL ORIGINS
Ancient Egyptians saw the dolphin as a symbol of Isis, goddess and patron of nature and magic. Some Native American tribes believe that dolphins are magical creatures and keepers of the breath of life, mainly because they breathe air but live in water. In classical Greece, the dolphin was called "King of Fishes" or "Arrow of the Sea." They were thought to be the guides of souls to the underworld and were a good omen for seafaring vessels.

GUIDING POWERS
If you're in need of a little joy, let the spirit of the dolphin be your guide. Dolphins are excellent companions if you're suffering from depression or stuck in a mental rut. If you're fresh out of brilliant ideas, the dolphin will illuminate the imaginary lightbulb above your head in a flash. It will show you how to smile through even the most difficult moments and to create a new rhythm in your life. And if your sex life has gone cold, the dolphin will show you how to bring back the sizzle via fun and frolic.

COMPANION ANIMALS
Ram (*sexuality*) and Hummingbird (*laughter*)

EAGLE
The Spiritual Seeker

PERSONALITY

The eagle is found all over the world, except for remote islands, and is one of the most sophisticated birds of prey, with incredible eyesight and mighty wings. Although it can soar to great altitudes, it can still see its quarry on the ground. The eagle is just as comfortable swooping down to use its powerful talons and fierce beak as it is soaring on the wind currents.

SPIRITUAL ORIGINS

The eagle is considered a sky or solar god in many different traditions. Many Native American tribes deeply revere the eagle; some believe only the holiest shamans are able to see it in its majestic glory. The eagle is thought to have tremendous power and is believed to live in both spiritual and earth realms. And eagle feathers are used all over the world as ceremonial instruments for shamans. In Scandinavian legend, the eagle sat at the top of the World Tree. The Finns believed the Supreme God could turn himself into an eagle. In Hindu tradition, the eagle was the bird of Indra, the god of thunder. So thoroughly revered is the eagle, that it is represented in the coats of arms of many countries.

GUIDING POWERS

The eagle can ease you into a state of inner grace. If you're longing to connect to the divine but lacking a conduit, the eagle is an excellent companion for your journey. It can teach you how to live in balance with earthly reality and celestial spirit. If you're learning to meditate, moving from one set of beliefs to another, or simply hungering for spirituality, link up with the eagle. It will help you to reconnect to your personal power.

COMPANION ANIMALS
Turtle (*stillness*) and Owl (*wisdom*)

ELEPHANT
The Peaceful Warrior

PERSONALITY
The largest living land animal, the elephant walks only five miles an hour—it needn't rush. . . . After all, the elephant has few enemies, as smaller animals are no match for its crushing strength. Its large and well-developed brain carries a keen intellect and what researchers qualify as very human emotions. Although this gentle giant is the strongest creature in the wild, it often relies on its brain instead of its brawn. Elephants are native to Africa and Asia.

SPIRITUAL ORIGINS
In the Hindu pantheon, Ganesha, the famous god with the head of an elephant, is known as the remover of obstacles—thousands of temples in India are dedicated to him. Also, according to Hindu mythology, Indra, god of thunder, rides a white elephant named Airavata. And Shiva's wife Radha is called "She-Elephant." Chinese Buddhists view the elephant as a wise and peaceful creature, exemplifying prudence and strength.

GUIDING POWERS
The elephant will serve you well when you're stuck in a jam. This slow-moving animal will show you how to push through mental, emotional, or physical barriers with little obvious effort. If you're feeling weak or powerless, call upon the elephant, the peaceful warrior, to gain the resilience you seek.

COMPANION ANIMALS
Crocodile *(power)* and Whale *(spiritual rebirth)*

FOX
The Cunning Trickster

PERSONALITY

The ingenious fox often plays dead for long periods, lying in wait for delicious birds to pop by and check it out. Once they get close enough, it pounces and dinner is served. He may be a trickster, but he mates for life. The long, lithe fox is nocturnal, hunting under cloak of night. Foxes are found in the Americas, Europe, Asia, and North Africa.

SPIRITUAL ORIGINS

Sumerians believed the fox was connected with the trickster god, Enki. The Japanese and Chinese both held that the fox could take human form simply for the sake of mischief. The Chinese thought fox sightings were indicators of the afterlife, while in Japan the fox symbolized the rice god, Inari. Northern Native Americans see the fox as a proud messenger, while Plains tribes see this wily creature as a con artist. The fox has always been associated with fire. In Scandinavia, the aurora borealis was known as the "Light of the Fox."

GUIDING POWERS

For getting out of a fix, no consort is better than the witty, cunning, adaptable fox. Its slyness can be a great example when you're faced with a career issue that requires particular savvy. Remember, even the most formidable opponent can be outfoxed. And if you need to do a little shape-shifting, let the fox be your guide. Its wicked sense of humor will lighten your mood when you're depressed. And the fox's fondness for causing mischief makes it an excellent teacher when you need to think your way outside of the box.

COMPANION ANIMALS
Hummingbird (*adaptability*) and Raccoon (*resourcefulness*)

HAWK
The Courageous Observer

PERSONALITY

The hawk appears to drift effortlessly on the wind. You'd never know that this creature is one of the most powerful on land or air by just watching it fly. As beautiful as it is, the hawk is keenly aware of everything in its purview. The hawk sees all and fears little, never missing a beat. Hawks are found all over the world, except for Antarctica.

SPIRITUAL ORIGINS

The Egyptian god Horus was depicted with a hawk's head on a human body. Also, due to its agility and swiftness, the hawk was considered a messenger of the Greek god Apollo. In Celtic oral traditions, the hawk is thought to be the oldest creature in the world.

GUIDING POWERS

If you feel like you're missing some important information, the hawk offers excellent counsel. The hawk will help you to find your way in the dark, turning shadow into light. If you're working hard on a project and facing burnout, the hawk will help you to find the energy to keep going. If you seek mental clarity on an emotional problem that you can't see your way around, the hawk will help you to zero in on the crux of the issue and work through it.

COMPANION ANIMALS
Bear (*creativity*) and Monkey (*precision*)

HORSE
The Gypsy Spirit

PERSONALITY

Horses long to run free. They are in their element when untethered, galloping gallantly across the plains without saddle or bridle. A wild horse is a wonder to behold; it's happiest without boundaries. The horse is native to North America, Asia, Europe, and Africa.

SPIRITUAL ORIGINS

The horse is one of the most storied creatures of the animal kingdom. To the Hindus, the horse is symbolic of wind, sea foam, the cosmos, fire, and light. The sun god Surya rode on a chariot harnessed to seven stallions. In Greek myth, Pegasus was a winged horse and the son of Poseidon, god of the sea. The horse was sacred to the Norse god Odin; he was often pictured riding one and sometimes shape-shifting into one. The astrological symbol for Sagittarius is half-man, half-horse, pointing toward freedom, philosophy, travel, and higher thinking.

GUIDING POWERS

When you feel like you need to move, get out, and break free of restriction, the horse is your ultimate spirit animal guide. If you've been stuck in a limiting mental sphere or emotionally constrained situation, consult the free-spirited horse. If you want to get away from it all by taking a vacation but are deterred by financial difficulties or personal obligations, the horse will show you how to dissolve boundaries and roam.

COMPANION ANIMALS
Butterfly *(freedom)* and Spider *(inspiration)*

HUMMINGBIRD
The Relentless Pleasure~Seeker

PERSONALITY

The only bird that can hover and fly backward, forward, up, or down, the hummingbird is incredibly adaptable. It is tiny and delicate, but can stop dead in its tracks while moving at full speed. Its wings beat fifty-five times a second; a speed any other creature in the animal kingdom finds impossible to beat. This incredible stamina allows the hummingbird to tirelessly seek out nectar from every source. These spritelike creatures are a direct link to pure, unadulterated happiness. Hummingbirds are found throughout the Americas.

SPIRITUAL ORIGINS

The Mayans thought of the hummingbird as a symbol of the Black Sun and the Fifth World, the era beginning after the present world ends in their cyclical understanding of time. They believed that dead warriors were reborn as hummingbirds. In Mexican folklore, the hummingbird symbolizes luck in love.

GUIDING POWERS

If you're in need of some serious joy, consult with the hummingbird. This creature shows us how to find hidden happiness and to see the best in people. It's the ideal spirit animal for those moments when you're overwhelmed by darkness and focused on the negatives. The hummingbird will show you how to find your sweet spot again. It takes perseverance and ingenuity to find your bliss once you've lost it. The hummingbird has endless stores of both, so if someone you love is feeling blue, call upon the hummingbird to bring back his or her laughter.

COMPANION ANIMALS
Monkey (*humor*) and Kangaroo (*abundance*)

JACKAL
The Savvy Scavenger

PERSONALITY

Jackals are crafty characters that do what they must to get by. They aren't necessarily the most beautiful or charming creatures, but they do possess shrewd
foraging skills. Jackals also know how to maneuver in groups. They are found
in Africa, India, and the Far East.

SPIRITUAL ORIGINS

The somewhat fearsome jackal was called the "lion's provider" in Africa because
its scavenging ways can lead other animals straight to a fresh kill. Jackals
are believed to conduct psychopomp work in a variety of cultures, meaning
they ferry souls to worlds beyond. Anubis, the Egyptian lord of the dead, had
the head of a jackal. And Kali, the Hindu goddess of destruction, was often
portrayed accompanied by jackals.

GUIDING POWERS

If you need to make something from nothing, you have much to learn from the
jackal. If you're stuck in the idea stage of a project and need to get practical,
the jackal will show you how to use the tools you have at hand, rather than
waiting for a flash of creative insight. If you're in a tight financial spot and
need to come up with some quick cash, the jackal can help you on your hunt.

COMPANION ANIMALS
Hawk *(agility)* and Bee *(industriousness)*

JAGUAR
The Fearless Liberator

PERSONALITY
These fierce fighters are not afraid to use their powerful jaws to slay their prey in a single motion. They are patient, however, and will follow a potential victim for many miles until the opportune moment to pounce reveals itself. Jaguars are extremely independent and like to live near bodies of water or in caves. They can be found in the Western Hemisphere, from Patagonia to Arizona.

SPIRITUAL ORIGINS
The Mayans and Aztecs made sacrifices to their jaguar gods. Tezcatlipoca, the Aztec warrior god, was regularly depicted as a jaguar. The Toltecs saw the jaguar as a symbol of rain and thunder and believed that the sun god transformed into a jaguar at night.

GUIDING POWERS
Jaguars show you how to walk the solitary path. Creative people often need the jaguar's help to get especially daunting projects started. Being alone with your true self can be painfully revealing: The jaguar encourages deep meditation and brutal unmasking of your purpose on earth. As you pull away layers and face your own darkness, the jaguar will show you how to go deep without fear.

COMPANION ANIMALS
Koala *(meditation)* and Scorpion *(intensity)*

KANGAROO
The Prosperous Risk~Taker

PERSONALITY

With their powerful feet and legs, kangaroos are able to leap more than thirty feet in a single bound. These marsupials are ultra-attentive mothers, known for keeping their babies safe and warm in their pouches until they are ready to explore the world solo. The kangaroo's long, thick tail is used for balancing. They are earthy, strong, and friendly creatures, found in Australia, Tasmania, and New Guinea.

SPIRITUAL ORIGINS

The kangaroo appears in a variety of Australian Aboriginal legends as a keeper of warmth and abundance, and sometimes as a hoarder. Although kangaroos are known for amazing jumping skills, they have their feet planted firmly on the ground.

GUIDING POWERS

Kangaroos teach us to leap forward into life instead of overanalyzing every step along the way. This spirit animal shows us how to have faith and take risks. Even if you feel completely bereft, the kangaroo's magnificent hoarding skills will show you how to access your own hidden resources. If you're feeling impoverished spiritually, creatively, or financially, the kangaroo can show you how to trust in abundance and believe that the universe will provide.

COMPANION ANIMALS
Buffalo *(wealth)* and Jaguar *(fearlessness)*

KOALA
The Single~Minded Hermit

PERSONALITY
The koala is a solitary animal that gains independence from its mother at
an early age. Koalas perch high in eucalyptus trees—their sole source of
sustenance—with a firm grip and solid footing. Although their eyesight is
poor, their hearing is exceptional. Masters of discrimination, these cute and
cuddly marsupials are beloved by humans, but they're not necessarily who we
think they are. They demand their personal space and would likely reject any
affection we tried to direct at them. Koalas are found in Eastern Australia.

SPIRITUAL ORIGINS
This endangered marsupial plays an integral role in the Aboriginal dreamtime
myth of creation. The word *Koala* is an Aboriginal word for "no drink," as they
drink very little water. Although they're known as koala "bears," these beloved
creatures are most closely related to the wombat, and do not share their genetic
heritage with the bear family.

GUIDING POWERS
No matter how much your friends and family might need you, sometimes you
simply crave time and space for yourself; the koala can show you how to make
this happen without guilt. The koala can be especially helpful during those
times when you need to focus and finish a project. The koala can also show
you how to pay attention to your own silences in the midst of a spiritual quest.
Eliminating external distractions is sometimes the only way to know the inner
self; with its keen hearing, this creature can show you how to tune into your
deepest needs.

COMPANION ANIMALS
Owl *(silence)* and Eagle *(divinity)*

LEOPARD

The Instinctual Warrior

PERSONALITY

As one of the most talented hunters in the animal kingdom, the leopard has a fearsome reputation. Leopards move silently and faster than most other animals, enabling them to get out of dangerous situations in the blink of an eye. The leopard's amazingly fast reaction time makes it seem as if it sees danger moments before it arrives. Big cats usually require tremendous water supplies, but the leopard is an anomaly—it can survive on very little. Leopards can be found all over Eurasia and Africa.

SPIRITUAL ORIGINS

The leopard is sacred to certain African tribes and is thought to inhabit the souls of the dead. The Chinese believed this creature represented ferocity and bravery. In Greek mythology, Dionysus, often associated with id and instinct, was sometimes depicted riding a leopard.

GUIDING POWERS

If you've built up anger or resentment after not getting your due, the leopard will teach you how to go directly after what you need. Listen to your gut—there's no need for hemming and hawing or feeling guilt. The leopard can show you how to get by on your instinct, without the benefit of coddling or nurturing from others. The leopard teaches you how to reconnect to your basic inner strength and, more importantly, how to put it to practical use.

COMPANION ANIMALS
Antelope *(breakthrough)* and Elephant *(strength)*

LION
The Confident Creator

PERSONALITY

Lions would rather roam the savanna with their pride than engage in battle with other animals. If provoked, of course, they will fight ferociously and protect their loved ones. They care for their young with great gentleness and more than enough patience, making for a beautiful family dynamic. Lions are mostly found in Africa, although they once roamed the Middle East and India.

SPIRITUAL ORIGINS

The lion is the symbol for Leo in the zodiac; Leo is the most dramatic and creative of the twelve signs—ruled by the sun and associated with royalty. The Egyptians linked the lion to power and wealth. The Chinese viewed the lion as a symbol of courage and strength. The cowardly lion of *Wizard of Oz* fame was inspired by this creature's long association with dignity, courage, and nobility.

GUIDING POWERS

The lion is your guide when you're in need of a little self-love. It teaches you not to be so hard on yourself and to relax, let go, and stop being such a workaholic. And lions don't frown upon primping: They'll tell you that, yes, it's more than okay to play hooky and book a massage. You're worth it. This relaxed confidence is the mark of the creative person you long to be—the one that takes a break when stressed instead of drowning in angst and neurosis.

COMPANION ANIMALS
Swan (*beauty*) and Hummingbird (*joy*)

LYNX
The Undercover Detective

PERSONALITY

The lynx is nocturnal, solitary, and territorial—and rarely seen by humans. Lynx have keen hearing, which makes them skilled hunters in the wild. If you get a glimpse of one, notice its expression: The lynx always appear to be wearing a secret, all-knowing smile, like the cat who swallowed the canary. The lynx can be found throughout the Western Hemisphere, and although it is now extinct in Europe, it still lives in certain regions of northern Asia.

SPIRITUAL ORIGINS

Some Native American tribes believe the lynx is a keeper of occult knowledge and able to solve mysteries. The Celts thought the lynx could help people divine the truth about those close to them. They also believed this spirit animal was clairvoyant.

GUIDING POWERS

The lynx will show you when to keep silent and when to share your knowledge. If you have a secret that you're dying to share, this spirit animal will guide you to someone that you can trust. If you need to unravel a perplexing mystery, the lynx will set you on the proper path. Most of all, the lynx can show you the power of truly listening, both to others and to your deepest self.

COMPANION ANIMALS
Raven (*secrets*) and Crocodile (*silence*)

MONKEY
The Charming Intellectual

PERSONALITY

Busiest during the day, these brilliant creatures are swift and graceful as can be. They have large brains, and they use them. Monkeys joyfully swing from tree branch to tree branch, seemingly without effort. Their long, lithe limbs and fantastic vision make them both agile and able. Monkeys are found in Africa, Asia, and South America.

SPIRITUAL ORIGINS

Hanuman, the Hindu monkey god, is a human-monkey hybrid thought to bestow longevity. He is one of the most famous and beloved gods of the Hindu pantheon, said to have rescued a kidnapped princess. Monkeys are one of the twelve animals in the Chinese zodiac and are thought to be inventive, intelligent, witty, lively, independent, versatile, humorous, generous, and charming.

GUIDING POWERS

The monkey is a great teacher when you're feeling out of sorts and flat-footed. If you've made a clumsy attempt to get someone's attention, submitted an admittedly weak proposal, or just aren't feeling up to snuff, the monkey can show you how to get your mojo back. If you need to get through many tasks with speed and precision, call upon the monkey.

COMPANION ANIMALS
Dolphin (*genius*) and Fox (*cunning*)

OWL
The Wise Hunter

PERSONALITY

Owls are solitary animals with keen eyesight and exceptional hearing. Nocturnal birds of prey, owls are fearsome hunters because of their long talons and strong beaks. Unlike many birds, introverted owls live a private existence. They fly noiselessly, swooping down without warning and scooping up vulnerable animals. As ruler of the night, the owl is not afraid to be alone, secure in the knowledge that its incomparable survival skills will always see it through. Owls are found all over the world, except for Antarctica and Greenland.

SPIRITUAL ORIGINS

As a symbol of both birth and the Great Goddess of the pre-Christian era, the wide-eyed owl was viewed as a protector of women and children by ancient cultures. This regal creature was a sacred icon wherever the power of the feminine was revered. Eventually, the owl became a harbinger of death for Babylonians, Egyptians, Hindus, and Celts. And Christianity considered the owl's "hoot" a call to summon witches. It wasn't all bad, though—Native American peoples revere the owl, and many tribes connect it to sacred knowledge.

GUIDING POWERS

Owls are ideal animal guides when you need to give birth to inner wisdom. They show us that with quiet wisdom comes great strength, and they offer insight from silence and dreams. Call upon your owl guide right before bed if you wish to reach a more mature understanding overnight. If you hunger for the hidden truths of your own psyche, or just require some time alone to think and meditate, invite the wise hunter.

COMPANION ANIMALS
Cat (*mysticism*) and Crab (*intuition*)

PEACOCK
The Confident Strutter

PERSONALITY

This stunning bird wears its feathers like a crown, unafraid to show off what nature has bestowed. Each of its dazzling feathers is tipped in iridescence, creating a metallic sheen unrivaled in the animal kingdom. They do preen, but how can they not? Peacocks can be found in the East Indies and Southeast Asia.

SPIRITUAL ORIGINS

Peacocks were sacred to ancient Babylonians and were associated with royalty in Persia. Revered in Japan and China, this beautiful bird symbolized high status in society. The peacock feather was an emblem of the Ming dynasty. Peacocks are thought to be lucky in India and are still allowed to walk the grounds of temples and royal gardens. Hindu icons Lakshmi, Saraswati, Brahma, and Kama all have been depicted riding a peacock.

GUIDING POWERS

If you long to be noticed for your talent but are shy about talking yourself up, call upon the dramatic peacock for a little bravery. This lovely bird will show you that confidence is not the same thing as vanity. We all need to show off our skills once in a while, and with the peacock's help you won't be afraid to invite an audience the next time you show off yours.

COMPANION ANIMALS
Lion *(hedonism)* and Swan *(confidence)*

RACCOON
The Masked Problem-Solver

PERSONALITY
Raccoons are adept scavengers: They can open cans, doors, and garbage pails.
Their long fingers work magic for them. They've adapted to our lifestyle and
manage to fit right in, sometimes living happily in or near cities. Rather
fastidious, they like to wash their hands before eating and prefer to sit high in
trees, observing the world around them and traveling in small groups at night.
The raccoon is found in North America.

SPIRITUAL ORIGINS
According to some Native American tribes, the raccoon is a scavenger extra-
ordinaire and is known as a symbol of masks and dexterity. The word *raccoon*
is thought to come from the Algonquin Indian word *arckunem*, meaning
"hand scratcher."

GUIDING POWERS
Resourcefulness is the raccoon's greatest gift. When faced with a complex
problem that you can't seem to find your way out of, consult with the adaptable
raccoon. This spirit animal will patiently guide you through all of the necessary
steps to reach your breakthrough. Once you solve the puzzle, the raccoon will
encourage you to let go and move on.

COMPANION ANIMALS
Elephant *(breakthrough)* and Hummingbird *(adaptability)*

RAM
The Passionate Self-Starter

PERSONALITY

In flocks of sheep, the size of a ram's horns helps to determine his place in the hierarchy, and the dominant male wins mating privileges. Rams are social animals, and their tendency to accept the herd mentality may have more to do with a sensual addiction to food than with any sort of inherent weakness. In fact, when threatened, they're known to stamp their feet and charge. Rams are found in Africa, Europe, the Americas, Australia, and New Zealand.

SPIRITUAL ORIGINS

The ram is the symbol of Aries, the very first sign of the zodiac, representing raw power, leadership, and bold, brash confidence. This sign is associated with fire and the warrior energy of Mars, ruling unbridled sexuality. The ram was sacred to Zeus, who was a seducer of both mortals and goddesses alike. And Pan, a lover of nymphs, was depicted as a man with horns and was associated with the ram.

GUIDING POWERS

If you're in need of some sensual healing, confer with the ram. Want to seduce someone? This creature will show you how to turn on any would-be companion. If the embers of your latest liaison are slowly dying, the ram will show you how to bring back the fire. When it comes to finding love, sometimes only boldness will do. The ram shows you the true shape of your power and provides endless solutions for any kind of loneliness.

COMPANION ANIMALS
Bull (*sensuality*) and Dolphin (*frolic*)

RAVEN
The Magic Messenger

PERSONALITY

Found throughout the northern hemisphere, ravens have a bad reputation, mainly because they feed on the dead. But ravens are bold, beautiful, and highly intelligent. They are great communicators, with a wide range of vocalizations; they can even mimic human speech. Ravens are able to imitate the sounds of wolves and coyotes, in effect calling them to the site of a dead animal to open the waiting carcass. Then the ravens swoop down for a ready-made meal.

SPIRITUAL ORIGINS

Some Native Americans believe the raven possesses the power to see the hidden. It is a bird of shamanic magic and has healing powers. Celtic goddesses and druidesses were often linked to ravens and were thought to have shape-shifting powers. Although the raven symbolizes death and change in many cultures, for the Chinese it signifies the sun. And in Norse mythology, Hugin and Munin were a pair of ravens that acted as messengers for Odin, the god of wisdom and magic.

GUIDING POWERS

When you feel like there's more to a situation than meets the eye, the raven can help unearth hidden elements. The raven will show you how to use your intuition to reveal obscure messages and secret transmissions. Spiritual journeying is the raven's domain; if you're trying to connect with a departed loved one or any entity from the "other side," the raven will be your willing translator.

COMPANION ANIMALS
Owl *(secrets)* and Cat *(mystery)*

SCORPION
The Vigilant Protector

PERSONALITY
These deadly, spiderlike creatures can survive freezing temperatures and desert heat alike. Scorpions are well known for their lethal stingers; less well known are their sophisticated pincers, with which they catch prey before killing it with their venom. Scorpions are willing to wait and observe prey until the most opportune moment to make their kill. And if they feel threatened, they'll stop at nothing to protect themselves. They will only sting humans or other non-prey when attacked or provoked. Scorpions are found in most parts of the world south of the 49th parallel, except for New Zealand.

SPIRITUAL ORIGINS
Scorpions are the symbol of the constellation of Scorpio, the eighth sign of the zodiac. This sign rules transformation, passion, and power plays. Scorpio is also thought to be the most intense of signs, often associated with revenge and occult arts. Scorpios are feared and revered, and known for their vigilant, intense focus. The Akkadians called the Scorpius constellation *Girtab*, meaning "the seizer." Set, the ancient Egyptian god of evil, was associated with the scorpion.

GUIDING POWERS
The scorpion is ready for anything, so call upon this spirit animal if you're feeling vulnerable or unprepared. If you've been hurt before and feel that you need a shield of protection, this is a powerful ally. If someone you love is under threat, the scorpion can arm you with the confidence needed to defend without fear.

COMPANION ANIMALS
Shark (*protection*) and Jaguar (*unmasking*)

SHARK
The Solitary Survivalist

PERSONALITY

Sharks have incredibly sharp senses: These predatory creatures are able to smell a single drop of blood in 50 million times as much water. They will generally leave other animals alone, however, if they're not hungry. But when pushed to their limits by hunger or stress, they will tear apart anything in their path. Sharks prefer to be alone much of the time and are frenzied when traveling in larger groups, swimming erratically and showing other signs of stress. Sharks are found in all oceans of the world, but they prefer warm seas.

SPIRITUAL ORIGINS

Sharks figure prominently in Polynesian mythology. In Hawaii, the legend of Kauhuhu, the shark god of Molokai, tells the story of a shark god who is friends with a priest. Tales of "shark men" also abound in Hawaiian mythology. Shark men are thought to change form from man to shark and to conceal their fierce shark jaws beneath their clothing while on land. Legend has it that the shark men warn people about the danger in the waters. Beachgoers ignore the shark men at their own peril—those who do are subsequently devoured in the sea.

GUIDING POWERS

The shark offers great protection when you're under threat. This creature will teach you the difference between lashing out arbitrarily and defending yourself out of true need. If you're in a situation in which boundaries seem unclear and you feel you may be under attack, call upon the shark for counsel.

COMPANION ANIMALS
Crab *(protection)* and Antelope *(survival)*

SNAKE
The Remarkable Reinventor

PERSONALITY

Despite their menacing reputation, snakes are beautiful, ancient, and enchanting. Although many of them will bite and release venom when threatened, that's not their preferred activity. They would rather slide through the grass unseen. Snakes are known for their seasonal molting, after which they are reborn as entirely new creatures, having literally shed their old skin. Snakes are found all over the world except for the coldest regions.

SPIRITUAL ORIGINS

Snakes are one of the most storied creatures on earth. From the Great Mother religions to the serpent in Genesis, snakes play the role of good and evil, solar and lunar, healing and poison, the earth and the underworld. Isis, the Egyptian goddess, was often depicted being carried by snakes. In ancient Greece, the goddess Gaea was the founder of the Delphic oracle (before Apollo subsumed it). She was called *Gaea Pelope*, female serpent. Ouroboros, the snake eating its own tail in the shape of an 8, is a symbol of eternity and completion. Some Native American traditions hold that all snakes are powerful, but the one with the most poisonous bite is the most powerful.

GUIDING POWERS

The snake is the great initiator of the animal kingdom. If you need to release the past and transition into a more positive place, the snake will help you to get there. This is an excellent companion to have when you're ready to shed an old relationship that once held great power over you. The snake is an animal of the eternal now; it shows you how to live in the present, exactly where you should always be.

COMPANION ANIMALS
Whale (*rebirth*) and Tiger (*meditation*)

SPIDER
The Creative Illusionist

PERSONALITY

Spiders are swift and fragile creatures that spin beautiful silken webs, seemingly out of nowhere. Yes, these webs ensnare smaller insects that the spider eats as prey, but their craftsmanship is still a wonder to behold. It seems as if spiderwebs are created to entrance and ensnare us with their beauty. Spiders are found throughout the world.

SPIRITUAL ORIGINS

Spiders are associated with the Hindu word *maya*, or "illusion." In a famous Greek myth, the goddess Athena turns Arachne into a spider after the latter boasts about her weaving skills. To the Japanese and some African tribes, the spider is a trickster. And some Native Americans call spider power the creative force of life.

GUIDING POWERS

If life feels a bit boring, and you're longing for some creative zest, call upon the spider. This is an excellent spirit animal companion when you're at the beginning of a project and need to jump-start your inspiration. If you're staring at a blank screen or a blank canvas, the spider will bring your sense of invention back. The spider can assist you whether you're a professional artist or are just in it for fun.

COMPANION ANIMALS
Monkey *(creativity)* and Swan *(beauty)*

SWAN
The Graceful Beauty

PERSONALITY

Swans mate for life. Long-necked and large, they are fast swimmers and glide gorgeously on the water. No other animal carries as much poise, dignity, and charm as the swan. And swans don't mind being observed; they seem to understand that they bring joy and wonder to voyeurs. In the children's fairy tale *The Ugly Duckling*, by Danish author Hans Christian Andersen, the distressed duckling is revealed as a beautiful swan in the final moments of the story. Swans are found in the Northern Hemisphere, Australia, and southern South America.

SPIRITUAL ORIGINS

In ancient Greece, the swan was an emblem of Aphrodite, goddess of love, and also of the Muses. In Roman mythology, swans were thought to pull Venus's chariot through the air. The heavenly nymphs of Hindu legend, called the *apsaras*, were often depicted as swans. And the goddess Devi is often shown riding a swan.

GUIDING POWERS

The swan will help you to get in touch with your inner beauty, especially in those moments when you're feeling your ugliest. If you're struggling with confidence regarding your outward appearance, the swan is the perfect companion. When the world is foreboding and your own image is burdened by dark shadows, the swan will bring you back into the light. Before you can truly love someone, you must learn to love yourself, warts and all. The lifelong mating traditions of the swan will guide you to an "inner marriage," readying you for a commitment in the real world.

COMPANION ANIMALS
Lion *(self-love)* and Peacock *(razzle-dazzle)*

Inner Beauty

TIGER
The Self-Directed Seeker

PERSONALITY

The tiger is a solitary hunter that stalks its prey patiently, rather than giving chase. It hunts in total silence and never gives away its position, waiting until the ideal moment to pounce. Tigers seem to need no other animal in the wild, living on their own terms and by their own timing. They are found mainly in Asia, from India up to Siberia. Their domain spans all the way to Caucasia, but no further into Europe.

SPIRITUAL ORIGINS

In China, the tiger is called "Lord of the Land Animals" and symbolizes the four directions: White tigers represent the west, symbolizing autumn. Blue tigers represent the east, symbolizing spring. Red tigers represent the south, symbolizing summer. And black tigers represent the north, symbolizing winter.

GUIDING POWERS

If you are prone to distraction and lack focus, the tiger can help you to zero in on what you must address. The tiger teaches meditation, simplicity, and the power of attending to immediate needs without drama. This spirit animal will bring you back to the present moment, where life is most potent and numinous, rather than allowing you to dwell in the past or focus relentlessly on the future.

COMPANION ANIMALS
Bear (*creative focus*) and Snake (*being in the now*)

TURTLE

The Calm, Cool, and Collected Contemplator

PERSONALITY
Turtles are herbivores that live both on land and in water. They deposit their eggs in holes they've dug for protection. Turtles move ever so slowly, contemplating each step. They have been around for eons and some can live for up to 150 years—it seems all they have is time. Turtles are found on every continent, except for Antarctica.

SPIRITUAL ORIGINS
The Hindus and the Chinese both believed the turtle supported the world. In Japan, it was thought that a turtle supported the Cosmic Mountains. According to some Native American traditions, the turtle is a symbol of the goddess, and its shell is symbolic of spiritual protection.

GUIDING POWERS
The turtle is a powerful ally in a 24/7 world. When you're stressed from texting and e-mailing and driving and meeting and talking every minute of every day, call upon the turtle. Like taking a vacation in the mountains or by the sea, connecting with the turtle forces us to remember that we live on earth, not online or in our offices. Call upon this spirit animal to get back in touch with your body and your internal world.

COMPANION ANIMALS
Deer (*centeredness*) and Lion (*relaxation*)